You Can Be An Influencer

Jon Alex Thomas

What, like it's hard?

Table of Contents

Contents

Chapter 1: Introduction to Influence 5
    Defining influence in the digital age 5
    Understanding the power and impact of influencers 7
    Exploring different types of influencers and their niches. 9

Chapter 2: Finding Your Passion 13
    Identifying your interests and expertise 13
    How to choose a niche that aligns with your passions ... 15
    Researching market demand and competition in your niche 18

Chapter 3: Building Your Personal Brand 21
    Crafting a unique personal brand identity 21
    Developing a compelling story and message 24
    Creating a cohesive brand aesthetic across platforms.. 26

Chapter 4: Content Creation Strategies 30
    Understanding the importance of high-quality content.. 30
    Exploring different types of content (e.g., photos, videos, written) 33
    Tips for creating engaging and shareable content 36

Chapter 5: Growing Your Audience 40
    Leveraging social media platforms to reach your target audience 40
    Strategies for increasing followers and engagement 43

Collaborating with other influencers and brands to expand your reach.. 46

Chapter 6: Monetizing Your Influence 50

Exploring different revenue streams for influencers (e.g., sponsored content, affiliate marketing, product sales).. 50

Negotiating deals with brands and advertisers............. 53

Building long-term partnerships and sustainable income streams 56

Chapter 7: Managing Your Online Presence 61

Dealing with trolls, negativity, and criticism................ 61

Maintaining authenticity and transparency with your audience 64

Balancing personal and professional boundaries.......... 67

Chapter 8: Evolving as an Influencer............................... 71

Staying relevant in a constantly changing digital landscape... 71

Adapting to new social media trends and platforms...... 74

Continuing education and professional development..... 77

Chapter 9: Case Studies and Success Stories 82

Interviews with successful influencers in various niches 82

Analyzing their strategies and key takeaways.............. 85

Inspiration and insights for aspiring influencers........... 89

Chapter 10: The Future of Influence................................. 94

Predictions for the future of influencer marketing 94

Emerging trends and technologies shaping the industry 98

    Opportunities and challenges for influencers in the years ahead.. 103

Epilogue: Your Journey to Influence 108

    Reflecting on your progress and achievements 108

    Setting new goals and aspirations for the future 112

    Encouragement and support for fellow influencers on their journey... 116

Conclusion 121

Chapter 1: Introduction to Influence

Defining influence in the digital age

In the digital age, influence has taken on a new dimension, transcending traditional boundaries and redefining how we connect, communicate, and consume information. At its core, influence in the digital era is about the ability to shape opinions, inspire action, and drive change through online platforms and communities.

One of the defining characteristics of influence in the digital age is its democratization. Unlike traditional forms of influence, which were often limited to celebrities, politicians, and other public figures, the rise of social media and digital content creation has empowered individuals from all walks of life to become influencers. Whether they're passionate about fashion, fitness, gaming, or gardening, anyone with an internet connection and a compelling message can build a following and wield influence in their chosen niche.

Another key aspect of influence in the digital age is its immediacy and reach. Social media platforms like Instagram, TikTok, YouTube, and Twitter enable influencers to connect with audiences on a global scale in real-time. With the click of a button, a single post or video can reach millions of people, sparking conversations, shaping trends, and driving engagement far beyond traditional media channels.

Moreover, influence in the digital age is inherently interactive and participatory. Unlike one-way communication channels like television or radio, social media platforms facilitate two-way dialogue between influencers and their followers. This direct and personal connection allows influencers to build authentic relationships with their audience, foster community, and cultivate trust—a crucial currency in an era of information overload and skepticism.

However, with great power comes great responsibility, and influence in the digital age is not without its challenges. The proliferation of fake news, misinformation, and algorithmic biases has raised concerns about the ethics and integrity of online influence. As such, influencers must navigate ethical dilemmas, uphold transparency, and exercise discernment in the content they create and promote.

In conclusion, influence in the digital age represents a paradigm shift in how we understand and wield power in the modern world. It is characterized by democratization, immediacy, interactivity, and responsibility. By harnessing the tools and platforms of the digital era, individuals have the opportunity to amplify their voices, effect change, and leave a lasting impact on society.

Understanding the power and impact of influencers

Understanding the power and impact of influencers requires a nuanced examination of their role in shaping public opinion, consumer behavior, and cultural trends in the digital age. From driving product sales to championing social causes, influencers wield significant influence across a wide range of domains.

First and foremost, influencers have the ability to sway consumer behavior and purchasing decisions. Through authentic storytelling, relatable content, and strategic partnerships with brands, influencers can effectively recommend products and services to their followers, often resulting in increased sales and brand awareness. This phenomenon, known as influencer marketing, has become a cornerstone of modern advertising strategies, allowing brands to reach highly targeted audiences in a more organic and engaging way than traditional advertising channels.

Moreover, influencers possess the power to shape cultural norms, values, and trends. By showcasing their lifestyles, preferences, and aspirations, influencers can influence societal attitudes and behaviors on a wide range of topics, from fashion and beauty standards to health and wellness practices. In this way, influencers serve as cultural tastemakers and trendsetters, driving conversations and shaping the zeitgeist in real-time through their content and social media presence.

Beyond consumerism and cultural influence, influencers also play a crucial role in raising awareness about social and environmental issues. With their large platforms and engaged audiences, influencers have the ability to amplify important messages, spark meaningful conversations, and mobilize support for various causes and campaigns. Whether it's promoting sustainability, advocating for social justice, or raising funds for charitable organizations, influencers can leverage their influence for positive impact and social change.

However, it's essential to recognize that the power and impact of influencers are not without their limitations and challenges. Influencers operate within a complex ecosystem of algorithms, market forces, and ethical considerations that can shape the reach and effectiveness of their influence. Moreover, the rise of influencer culture has also sparked debates about authenticity, transparency, and the commodification of personal experiences and relationships.

In conclusion, influencers wield significant power and impact in the digital age, shaping consumer behavior, cultural trends, and social discourse in profound ways. By understanding and harnessing the potential of influencers, brands, organizations, and individuals can leverage their influence to drive meaningful change and create a positive impact on society.

Exploring different types of influencers and their niches

Exploring the diverse landscape of influencers reveals a rich tapestry of personalities, passions, and niches, each with its unique audience and appeal. From beauty gurus to tech enthusiasts, influencers span a wide spectrum of interests and expertise, catering to the varied tastes and preferences of their followers. Here's a glimpse into some of the different types of influencers and the niches they inhabit:

1. Lifestyle Influencers:

   - Lifestyle influencers curate content around their everyday lives, sharing insights, tips, and experiences related to topics such as travel, home decor, fashion, and wellness. They often showcase aspirational lifestyles and offer inspiration and advice to their followers seeking to emulate their aesthetic and lifestyle choices.

2. Beauty and Fashion Influencers:

   - Beauty and fashion influencers specialize in all things glamour and style, providing tutorials, reviews, and recommendations for skincare, makeup, haircare, and fashion trends. With their expertise and creativity, they inspire followers to experiment with new looks and products while promoting brands and collaborations within the beauty and fashion industry.

3. Fitness and Wellness Influencers:

   - Fitness and wellness influencers focus on promoting health, fitness, and self-care practices, sharing workout routines, nutrition tips, and motivational content to help followers lead healthier lifestyles. They often document their own fitness journeys and transformations, serving as role models and sources of inspiration for their audience.

4. Travel Influencers:

   - Travel influencers are globetrotters who document their adventures, experiences, and recommendations from destinations around the world. Through stunning photography, captivating stories, and travel guides, they inspire wanderlust and provide valuable insights for followers planning their own trips and adventures.

5. Food and Cooking Influencers:

   - Food and cooking influencers delight audiences with mouthwatering recipes, cooking tutorials, and restaurant recommendations. They showcase their culinary creations, share cooking tips and techniques, and highlight food culture and traditions from around the globe, catering to foodies and home cooks alike.

6. Gaming and Esports Influencers:

   - Gaming and esports influencers are passionate gamers who create content around video games, streaming gameplay, providing commentary, and engaging with their community of fellow gamers. With their expertise and charisma, they entertain, educate, and inspire audiences while promoting gaming culture and products.

7. Parenting and Family Influencers:

   - Parenting and family influencers share their journey through parenthood, offering parenting advice, family-friendly activities, and insights into family life. They create relatable content that resonates with parents and caregivers, addressing common challenges and celebrating the joys of raising children.

8. Tech and Innovation Influencers:

   - Tech and innovation influencers are at the forefront of the digital revolution, sharing insights, reviews, and updates on the latest gadgets, technology trends, and innovations. They cater to tech enthusiasts and early adopters, providing valuable information and recommendations to help their followers stay informed and empowered in the ever-evolving world of technology.

These are just a few examples of the diverse range of influencers and niches that exist in the digital landscape. Each influencer brings their unique voice, perspective, and expertise to their respective niche, connecting with audiences and building communities around shared interests and passions. As the influencer industry continues to evolve, new niches and opportunities are constantly emerging, reflecting the dynamic and ever-changing nature of digital influence.

Chapter 2: Finding Your Passion

Identifying your interests and expertise

Identifying your interests and expertise is the crucial first step on the journey to becoming an influencer. Your passions and knowledge are the foundation upon which you'll build your personal brand and connect with your audience authentically. Here are some steps to help you identify your interests and expertise:

1. Self-Reflection:

Take some time to reflect on your interests, hobbies, and experiences. What are the activities that you enjoy doing in your free time? What topics or subjects do you find yourself constantly reading or learning about? Consider your past experiences, skills, and achievements—what are you passionate about, and what are you good at?

2. Make a List:

Create a list of topics or niches that align with your interests and expertise. This could include anything from fashion and beauty to travel, fitness, technology, food, parenting, or sustainability. Don't limit yourself—brainstorm as many ideas as possible, and don't be afraid to explore unconventional or niche interests.

3. Research and Explore:

Once you have your list, conduct research to explore each potential niche further. Look into popular influencers and content creators within each niche to see what type of content resonates with their audience and how they position themselves within the industry. Pay attention to trends, audience demographics, and engagement levels to gauge the potential viability of each niche.

4. Evaluate Your Passion and Knowledge:

Assess your level of passion and knowledge for each niche on your list. Ask yourself: which topics am I genuinely passionate about? Where do I have the most expertise or experience? Consider factors such as your ability to create engaging content, connect with your audience authentically, and stay motivated and committed in the long term.

5. Narrow Down Your Options:

After careful consideration, narrow down your list to a few select niches that resonate with you the most and align with your interests, expertise, and goals. Focus on niches where you can genuinely add value, stand out from the competition, and build a loyal and engaged audience.

6. Test and Experiment:

Once you've identified your primary niche(s), start creating content and engaging with your audience to test the waters and see how they respond. Experiment with different types of content, platforms, and strategies to find what works best for you and resonates with your audience. Pay attention to feedback, metrics, and audience interactions to refine your approach over time.

Remember that identifying your interests and expertise is an ongoing process, and it's okay to evolve and pivot as you gain more experience and insights. Stay true to yourself, stay curious, and don't be afraid to explore new opportunities and niches along the way. Your passion and authenticity are your greatest assets as an influencer, so embrace them wholeheartedly as you embark on your journey.

How to choose a niche that aligns with your passions

Choosing a niche that aligns with your passions is essential for building a successful and fulfilling influencer career. When you're passionate about your niche, creating content becomes more enjoyable, authentic, and sustainable in the long run. Here's how to choose a niche that resonates with your passions:

1. Identify Your Passions:

Take some time to reflect on your interests, hobbies, and areas of expertise. What are the activities or topics that excite you the most? What do you enjoy doing in your free time? Consider both your current passions and those that have been consistent throughout your life.

2. Assess Your Skills and Knowledge:

Evaluate your skills, knowledge, and experiences related to each of your passions. What are you good at? What do you have expertise in? Consider your professional background, educational qualifications, hobbies, and personal experiences. Your unique skills and expertise will set you apart in your chosen niche.

3. Research Potential Niches:

Once you have a list of passions and interests, research potential niches within each of them. Look into the size of the audience, competition, and engagement levels within each niche. Consider factors such as market demand, audience demographics, and growth potential to gauge the viability of each niche.

4. Consider Audience Alignment:

Evaluate how well each niche aligns with your target audience's interests, preferences, and demographics. Choose a niche where there is a natural overlap between your passions and your audience's interests. You'll be more successful in connecting with and engaging your audience when you're genuinely passionate about the content you create.

5. Explore Your Unique Angle:

Think about how you can bring your unique perspective, voice, and expertise to your chosen niche. Consider what sets you apart from other influencers in the same niche and how you can leverage your personality, experiences, and insights to create compelling and differentiated content.

6. Test and Validate:

Before committing fully to a niche, test the waters by creating some content and engaging with your audience to see how they respond. Experiment with different topics, formats, and platforms to gauge audience interest and feedback. Pay attention to metrics such as engagement rates, follower growth, and audience demographics to validate your niche choice.

7. Listen to Your Instincts:

Trust your instincts and intuition when choosing a niche. Follow your heart and pursue niches that genuinely excite and inspire you. Remember that passion is contagious, and when you're passionate about your niche, your enthusiasm will resonate with your audience and draw them in.

By choosing a niche that aligns with your passions, you'll not only enjoy the process of creating content but also build a loyal and engaged audience who shares your enthusiasm. Stay true to yourself, stay curious, and embrace the journey of exploring and sharing your passions with the world as an influencer.

Researching market demand and competition in your niche

Researching market demand and competition in your niche is crucial for understanding the landscape you'll be operating in as an influencer. By gaining insights into audience needs, preferences, and competitors, you can identify opportunities, refine your content strategy, and differentiate yourself in the market. Here's how to conduct effective research:

1. Define Your Niche:

Clearly define the niche or topic you're interested in focusing on as an influencer. Be specific about the subject matter, audience demographics, and the unique angle or perspective you bring to the table. This will help narrow down your research focus and identify relevant competitors and audience segments.

2. Identify Competitors:

Use social media platforms, search engines, and influencer marketing tools to identify competitors within your niche. Look for influencers who create similar content, target a similar audience, or operate in related niches. Pay attention to their content, engagement levels, audience demographics, and partnerships with brands.

3. Analyze Audience Engagement:

Evaluate the engagement levels of your competitors' content to gauge audience interest and preferences. Look at metrics such as likes, comments, shares, and views to understand which types of content resonate the most with their audience. Pay attention to recurring themes, trends, and topics that generate high levels of engagement.

4. Research Audience Demographics:

Use audience analytics tools and social media insights to gather data on your competitors' audience demographics. Understand who their followers are in terms of age, gender, location, interests, and behavior patterns. This will help you identify opportunities to target specific audience segments or tailor your content to meet their needs.

5. Assess Content Trends:

Stay up-to-date on content trends and industry developments within your niche. Monitor popular hashtags, trending topics, and viral content to identify emerging trends and opportunities for content creation. Look for gaps or underserved areas within the market where you can carve out a niche for yourself.

6. Evaluate Brand Partnerships:

Take note of the brand partnerships and sponsorships your competitors have secured within your niche. Analyze the types of brands they collaborate with, the frequency of partnerships, and the nature of sponsored content. This can provide insights into potential brand opportunities and revenue streams for your own influencer business.

7. Conduct Keyword Research:

Use keyword research tools to identify relevant keywords and search terms related to your niche. Understand the search volume, competition, and trends associated with these keywords to optimize your content for search engines and attract organic traffic to your platforms.

8. Gather Feedback:

Engage with your audience and gather feedback through surveys, polls, and direct interactions. Ask them about their preferences, interests, and pain points related to your niche. Use this feedback to refine your content strategy, address audience needs, and stay relevant in the ever-changing influencer landscape.

By conducting thorough research on market demand and competition in your niche, you'll be better equipped to position yourself effectively, create engaging content, and build a loyal and engaged audience as an influencer. Stay informed, stay curious, and adapt your strategy based on evolving market trends and audience preferences.

Chapter 3: Building Your Personal Brand

Crafting a unique personal brand identity

Crafting a unique personal brand identity is essential for standing out in a crowded influencer landscape and building a loyal and engaged audience. Your personal brand is more than just your content—it's the essence of who you are, what you stand for, and the value you offer to your audience. Here's how to create a distinctive personal brand identity:

1. Define Your Brand Values and Mission:

Start by defining the core values and mission that guide your personal brand. What do you believe in? What causes or issues are you passionate about? Your values and mission will serve as the foundation of your brand identity, shaping your content, voice, and overall message.

2. Identify Your Unique Selling Proposition (USP):

Determine what sets you apart from other influencers in your niche. What makes you unique? What special skills, experiences, or insights do you bring to the table? Your unique selling proposition (USP) should be a clear and compelling reason why people should follow and engage with your content.

3. Develop Your Brand Persona:

Create a distinct brand persona that reflects your personality, style, and voice. Are you witty and humorous, or serious and authoritative? Do you prefer a casual and conversational tone, or a more polished and professional demeanor? Your brand persona should resonate with your target audience and align with your niche and content theme.

4. Establish Visual Branding Elements:

Choose visual branding elements that represent your personal brand identity, such as a logo, color palette, typography, and imagery style. These elements should be consistent across all your platforms and content, helping to create a cohesive and recognizable brand identity that stands out in the digital landscape.

5. Create Compelling Content:

Develop content that aligns with your brand values, mission, and persona. Share stories, insights, and experiences that showcase your expertise, personality, and authenticity. Experiment with different formats, such as videos, blog posts, and social media posts, to engage your audience and keep them coming back for more.

6. Be Authentic and Transparent:

Authenticity and transparency are key pillars of a strong personal brand. Be genuine and honest in your interactions with your audience, sharing both your successes and struggles openly. Build trust by staying true to your values and maintaining consistency in your messaging and behavior.

7. Engage and Connect with Your Audience:

Foster meaningful connections with your audience by engaging with them regularly and responding to comments, messages, and feedback. Show appreciation for their support and involvement in your community, and involve them in your content creation process by asking for their input and suggestions.

8. Evolve and Adapt:

Personal branding is an ongoing process of self-discovery, growth, and refinement. Stay open to feedback, learn from your experiences, and adapt your brand strategy as needed to stay relevant and authentic in the ever-changing influencer landscape.

By crafting a unique personal brand identity that reflects your values, personality, and expertise, you'll attract like-minded followers who resonate with your message and vision. Stay true to yourself, stay consistent, and let your authentic voice shine through in everything you do as an influencer.

Developing a compelling story and message

Developing a compelling story and message is essential for connecting with your audience on a deeper level, resonating with their emotions, and inspiring them to engage with your content. Your story is what sets you apart from other influencers and creates a memorable and authentic brand identity. Here's how to develop a compelling story and message:

1. Know Your Why:

Start by reflecting on your personal journey, experiences, and motivations. What inspired you to become an influencer? What drives you to create content and share your message with others? Your "why" is the foundation of your story, serving as the guiding force behind your brand and content.

2. Define Your Brand Story:

Craft a narrative that tells the story of who you are, where you come from, and what you stand for. Share key moments, challenges, and milestones from your life that have shaped your identity and values. Your brand story should be authentic, relatable, and emotionally compelling, drawing your audience in and fostering a sense of connection and empathy.

3. Highlight Your Values and Mission:

Communicate your core values and mission through your brand story and messaging. What do you believe in? What causes or issues are you passionate about? Your values and mission should be woven into the fabric of your content, guiding your decisions and actions as an influencer.

4. Be Vulnerable and Authentic:

Embrace vulnerability and authenticity in sharing your story and experiences with your audience. Be open and honest about your successes, failures, and challenges, allowing your audience to see the real person behind the brand. Vulnerability fosters trust and relatability, strengthening the bond between you and your followers.

5. Connect Emotionally:

Appeal to your audience's emotions by sharing stories and anecdotes that resonate with their own experiences and aspirations. Use storytelling techniques such as vivid imagery, sensory details, and relatable characters to bring your message to life and evoke empathy, inspiration, or nostalgia.

6. Provide Solutions and Inspiration:

Offer practical advice, insights, or solutions that align with your brand story and values. Share lessons learned, tips, and strategies that empower your audience to overcome challenges, pursue their passions, or achieve their goals. Inspire and motivate your followers to take action and make positive changes in their lives.

7. Consistency and Cohesion:

Ensure consistency and cohesion in your brand story and messaging across all your platforms and content. Your story should be reflected in your bio, captions, visuals, and overall brand aesthetic, creating a cohesive and unified brand identity that resonates with your audience.

8. Listen and Adapt:

Pay attention to feedback, comments, and reactions from your audience, and be willing to adapt and evolve your story and messaging based on their interests and needs. Stay authentic and true to your values, but also remain flexible and responsive to the evolving preferences of your audience.

By developing a compelling story and message that reflects your values, experiences, and aspirations, you'll create a powerful connection with your audience and leave a lasting impact as an influencer. Stay true to your authentic voice, share your story with passion and purpose, and watch as your audience engages and grows along with you.

Creating a cohesive brand aesthetic across platforms

Creating a cohesive brand aesthetic across platforms is essential for building a strong and recognizable personal brand as an influencer. A cohesive brand aesthetic helps to establish visual consistency, reinforce your brand identity, and create a memorable and engaging experience for your audience. Here's how to create a cohesive brand aesthetic across platforms:

1. Define Your Brand Identity:

Start by defining your brand identity, including your core values, mission, and target audience. Consider the emotions, themes, and messages you want to convey through your brand, as well as your unique personality and style. Your brand identity will serve as the foundation for your aesthetic choices.

2. Choose Your Visual Elements:

Select key visual elements that reflect your brand identity and resonate with your audience. This includes your color palette, typography, imagery style, and graphic elements. Choose colors, fonts, and imagery that evoke the desired mood, tone, and aesthetic of your brand.

3. Create a Style Guide:

Develop a style guide that outlines your brand's visual elements and provides guidelines for their use across platforms. Include specifications for colors, fonts, image treatments, and graphic elements, as well as examples of how they should be applied in different contexts. A style guide ensures consistency and coherence in your brand's visual representation.

4. Design Your Brand Assets:

Design branded assets such as logos, graphics, and templates that reflect your brand identity and aesthetic. These assets will serve as visual cues and reinforcement of your brand across platforms. Use consistent design elements and imagery to create a cohesive and unified brand experience.

5. Maintain Consistent Branding:

Apply your brand aesthetic consistently across all your platforms and content channels. Use the same color palette, fonts, and imagery styles in your website, social media profiles, blog, videos, and other content. Consistent branding reinforces your brand identity and helps to build brand recognition and recall.

6. Curate Your Content:

Curate your content with your brand aesthetic in mind, selecting visuals and imagery that align with your brand identity and messaging. Choose photos, videos, and graphics that reflect your brand values, evoke the desired emotions, and appeal to your target audience. Maintain a consistent visual tone and style in your content creation process.

7. Optimize for Each Platform:

Tailor your brand aesthetic to fit the specifications and requirements of each platform you're active on. This may include optimizing image sizes and formats, adjusting content layouts, and adapting visual styles to suit the platform's audience and user experience. While maintaining consistency, be mindful of platform-specific nuances and trends.

8. Evolve and Adapt:

As your brand grows and evolves, be open to refining and adapting your brand aesthetic to reflect changes in your audience, industry trends, or personal preferences. Periodically review your branding elements and content to ensure they remain aligned with your brand identity and goals.

By creating a cohesive brand aesthetic across platforms, you'll establish a strong and recognizable visual presence that resonates with your audience and reinforces your brand identity as an influencer. Stay true to your brand values and vision, and let your unique aesthetic shine through in everything you do.

Chapter 4: Content Creation Strategies

Understanding the importance of high-quality content

Understanding the importance of high-quality content is fundamental for success as an influencer in today's digital landscape. High-quality content not only attracts and engages your audience but also builds trust, credibility, and loyalty over time. Here's why high-quality content is essential:

1. Captures Attention:

In a sea of content vying for attention, high-quality content stands out. Whether it's a beautifully composed photo, a well-produced video, or a thought-provoking blog post, high-quality content grabs the viewer's attention and compels them to engage with it further.

2. Builds Trust and Credibility:

High-quality content demonstrates your expertise, professionalism, and dedication to your craft. It shows that you care about delivering value to your audience and are committed to maintaining a high standard of quality. This builds trust and credibility with your audience, making them more likely to listen to your recommendations and engage with your brand.

3. Enhances Brand Image:

Your content is a reflection of your personal brand and values. High-quality content helps to enhance your brand image and perception, positioning you as a reputable and authoritative figure within your niche. It communicates professionalism, attention to detail, and a commitment to excellence, which can positively impact how your audience perceives you and your brand.

4. Increases Engagement and Interaction:

High-quality content is more engaging and interactive, encouraging your audience to like, comment, share, and participate in conversations around your content. Quality visuals, compelling storytelling, and valuable insights prompt deeper engagement and foster meaningful connections with your audience.

5. Drives Traffic and Conversions:

High-quality content has the power to drive traffic to your website, social media profiles, and other online platforms. Whether it's through SEO-optimized blog posts, eye-catching social media posts, or engaging videos, quality content attracts visitors and encourages them to explore further, ultimately leading to conversions and sales.

6. Positions You as an Influencer:

Consistently producing high-quality content establishes you as a thought leader and influencer within your niche. It demonstrates your expertise, authority, and passion for your subject matter, earning you respect and recognition from your peers and industry stakeholders.

7. Improves SEO and Visibility:

High-quality content is more likely to be discovered and ranked favorably by search engines, increasing your visibility and organic reach. By creating valuable, relevant, and well-optimized content, you can improve your SEO performance and attract a wider audience to your platforms.

8. Fosters Long-Term Relationships:

Building a successful influencer career is not just about acquiring followers—it's about nurturing long-term relationships with your audience. High-quality content fosters loyalty and retention by consistently delivering value and meeting the needs and expectations of your audience.

In conclusion, high-quality content is the cornerstone of a successful influencer strategy. It sets you apart from the competition, builds trust and credibility with your audience, and drives engagement, traffic, and conversions. By prioritizing quality in your content creation efforts, you can establish yourself as a respected and influential voice within your niche, paving the way for long-term success and impact as an influencer.

Exploring different types of content (e.g., photos, videos, written)

Exploring different types of content is essential for diversifying your influencer strategy, reaching a wider audience, and engaging with your followers across various platforms and channels. Each type of content offers unique advantages and appeals to different preferences and consumption habits. Here's an overview of some common types of content:

1. Photos:

Photos are a visually engaging and versatile form of content that can be shared across a variety of platforms, including Instagram, Facebook, Twitter, and Pinterest. Whether it's stunning landscapes, stylish fashion shots, or mouthwatering food photography, compelling photos can capture attention and evoke emotions with a single glance.

2. Videos:

Videos are one of the most engaging and immersive forms of content, allowing you to tell stories, demonstrate products, and connect with your audience in a dynamic and interactive way. Video content can take many forms, including vlogs, tutorials, reviews, interviews, and behind-the-scenes footage. Platforms like YouTube, TikTok, Instagram Reels, and Facebook Watch are popular for sharing video content.

3. Written Content:

Written content encompasses blog posts, articles, captions, and long-form social media posts. It allows you to convey information, express opinions, and engage with your audience through written language. Written content is often used for in-depth exploration of topics, sharing personal stories, providing educational insights, or sparking discussions on social issues.

4. Live Streams:

Live streaming allows you to broadcast real-time video content to your audience, enabling immediate interaction and engagement. Platforms like Instagram Live, Facebook Live, YouTube Live, and Twitch are popular for hosting live streams. Live streams can include Q&A sessions, product launches, behind-the-scenes glimpses, tutorials, and interactive challenges.

5. Stories:

Stories are short-lived, ephemeral content that disappears after 24 hours, making them ideal for sharing casual, in-the-moment updates with your audience. Platforms like Instagram, Facebook, Snapchat, and WhatsApp offer story features that allow you to share photos, videos, text, and interactive stickers with your followers.

6. Podcasts:

Podcasts are audio-based content that allows you to share information, interviews, discussions, and storytelling with your audience in an accessible and convenient format. Podcasting platforms like Apple Podcasts, Spotify, Google Podcasts, and Stitcher enable you to reach listeners on-the-go and connect with them through spoken-word content.

7. Infographics:

Infographics combine visual elements, text, and data to present information in a visually appealing and easy-to-understand format. They're perfect for conveying complex concepts, statistics, or step-by-step guides in a concise and engaging manner. Infographics can be shared on social media, websites, blogs, and presentations.

8. Interactive Content:

Interactive content encourages active engagement and participation from your audience, such as quizzes, polls, surveys, and interactive challenges. Platforms like Instagram, Facebook, and Twitter offer features that allow you to create and share interactive content to spark conversations and gather feedback from your followers.

By exploring and incorporating different types of content into your influencer strategy, you can keep your audience engaged, cater to diverse preferences, and maximize your reach and impact across various platforms and channels. Experiment with different formats, analyze performance metrics, and listen to feedback from your audience to refine your content strategy and create meaningful connections with your followers.

Tips for creating engaging and shareable content

Creating engaging and shareable content is key to building a loyal and active audience as an influencer. When your content resonates with your audience and compels them to share it with others, you'll see increased visibility, reach, and engagement. Here are some tips for creating content that captivates your audience and encourages sharing:

1. Know Your Audience:

Understand who your audience is, what they're interested in, and what resonates with them. Tailor your content to address their needs, preferences, and pain points. By creating content that speaks directly to your audience, you'll increase the likelihood of engagement and sharing.

2. Tell Compelling Stories:

Storytelling is a powerful way to engage your audience emotionally and draw them into your content. Share personal anecdotes, experiences, or case studies that resonate with your audience and illustrate key messages or themes. Use storytelling techniques such as vivid imagery, relatable characters, and suspense to keep your audience captivated.

3. Create Valuable and Useful Content:

Offer content that provides value, solves problems, or entertains your audience. Whether it's educational tutorials, practical tips, or entertaining anecdotes, focus on creating content that enriches your audience's lives and adds value to their day. When your content is helpful and informative, people are more likely to share it with others.

4. Embrace Visual Appeal:

Visual content is highly engaging and shareable, so invest in high-quality visuals that capture attention and tell your story effectively. Use eye-catching photos, videos, graphics, and infographics to convey your message in a visually appealing way. Pay attention to composition, color, and aesthetics to create content that stands out in the feed.

5. Spark Emotion:

Aim to evoke emotion in your audience through your content—whether it's joy, laughter, inspiration, empathy, or awe. Emotional content resonates with people on a deeper level and compels them to take action, whether it's liking, commenting, or sharing your content with others. Use storytelling, humor, or heartfelt messages to tap into your audience's emotions.

6. Encourage Engagement:

Prompt your audience to engage with your content by asking questions, inviting opinions, or encouraging participation. Create interactive content such as polls, quizzes, challenges, or user-generated content campaigns that encourage active engagement and interaction. When people feel involved and valued, they're more likely to share your content with their networks.

7. Optimize for Sharing:

Make it easy for people to share your content by including social sharing buttons, clickable links, and clear calls-to-action in your posts. Encourage sharing by explicitly asking your audience to share your content if they find it valuable or interesting. Leverage popular hashtags, trends, and viral topics to increase the chances of your content being shared.

8. Be Authentic and Genuine:

Authenticity is key to building trust and rapport with your audience. Be genuine, transparent, and true to yourself in your content creation process. Share your passions, interests, and personality authentically, and let your unique voice and perspective shine through in everything you do. Authentic content resonates with people and encourages them to share it with others who may relate to or appreciate your authenticity.

By incorporating these tips into your content creation strategy, you can create engaging and shareable content that resonates with your audience, sparks conversations, and amplifies your reach and impact as an influencer. Experiment with different formats, styles, and topics, and listen to feedback from your audience to refine your approach and create content that truly connects with your followers.

Chapter 5: Growing Your Audience

Leveraging social media platforms to reach your target audience

Leveraging social media platforms is essential for reaching your target audience as an influencer. With billions of users worldwide, social media offers unparalleled opportunities to connect with your audience, build relationships, and grow your brand presence. Here are some tips for effectively leveraging social media platforms to reach your target audience:

1. Identify Your Target Audience:

Start by defining who your target audience is—what are their demographics, interests, behaviors, and preferences? Understanding your audience allows you to tailor your content and messaging to resonate with their needs and interests.

2. Choose the Right Platforms:

Select social media platforms that align with your target audience's demographics and preferences. For example, if your audience is predominantly young and visually-oriented, platforms like Instagram, TikTok, and Snapchat may be ideal. If your audience is more professional and business-oriented, platforms like LinkedIn may be more suitable.

3. Optimize Your Profiles:

Ensure that your social media profiles are fully optimized with relevant information, compelling visuals, and clear messaging. Use high-quality profile pictures, cover photos, and bio descriptions to create a strong first impression and communicate your brand identity effectively.

4. Create Engaging Content:

Produce content that is engaging, relevant, and valuable to your audience. Experiment with different formats, such as photos, videos, stories, and live streams, to keep your content fresh and diverse. Use compelling visuals, storytelling techniques, and interactive elements to capture attention and prompt engagement.

5. Post Consistently:

Maintain a consistent posting schedule to keep your audience engaged and active. Regularly share new content, updates, and insights to stay top-of-mind and maintain momentum on social media. Use scheduling tools and content calendars to plan and organize your posts in advance.

6. Engage with Your Audience:

Foster meaningful interactions with your audience by responding to comments, messages, and mentions promptly. Encourage conversations, ask questions, and solicit feedback to keep your audience engaged and involved. Show appreciation for your followers' support and participation in your community.

7. Use Hashtags and Keywords:

Incorporate relevant hashtags and keywords into your posts to increase visibility and reach on social media. Research popular hashtags and keywords within your niche and include them strategically in your content to attract new followers and expand your audience reach.

8. Collaborate with Influencers and Brands:

Collaborate with other influencers and brands within your niche to amplify your reach and exposure on social media. Partnering with like-minded influencers and brands allows you to tap into their audience and leverage their credibility and influence to grow your own following.

9. Analyze and Iterate:

Monitor your social media analytics regularly to track your performance, identify trends, and gain insights into what resonates with your audience. Use this data to optimize your content strategy, refine your messaging, and experiment with new approaches to reach and engage your target audience more effectively.

By leveraging social media platforms strategically and authentically, you can reach, engage, and build relationships with your target audience, ultimately growing your influence and impact as an influencer. Stay true to your brand identity, experiment with different tactics, and adapt to the evolving preferences and trends of your audience to maximize your success on social media.

Strategies for increasing followers and engagement

Increasing followers and engagement is a common goal for influencers looking to grow their presence and influence on social media. By implementing strategic tactics and engaging with your audience authentically, you can attract new followers and cultivate a loyal and engaged community. Here are some effective strategies for increasing followers and engagement:

1. Define Your Niche and Target Audience:

   Clearly define your niche and target audience to attract followers who are genuinely interested in your content. Focus on a specific topic, theme, or industry that aligns with your interests, expertise, and audience demographics. Tailor your content to address the needs, preferences, and pain points of your target audience.

2. Create High-Quality Content:

Produce high-quality, visually appealing content that captures attention and resonates with your audience. Use high-resolution photos, professionally edited videos, and compelling storytelling techniques to stand out in the crowded social media landscape. Experiment with different formats, styles, and topics to keep your content fresh and engaging.

3. Post Consistently and Strategically:

Maintain a consistent posting schedule to keep your audience engaged and active. Experiment with different posting times and frequencies to determine when your audience is most active and responsive. Use scheduling tools and content calendars to plan and organize your posts in advance for maximum impact.

4. Use Hashtags and Keywords:

Incorporate relevant hashtags and keywords into your posts to increase visibility and reach on social media. Research popular hashtags and keywords within your niche and include them strategically in your content to attract new followers and expand your audience reach. Use niche-specific hashtags to target a more relevant audience.

5. Engage with Your Audience:

Foster meaningful interactions with your audience by responding to comments, messages, and mentions promptly.

Encourage conversations, ask questions, and solicit feedback to keep your audience engaged and involved. Show appreciation for your followers' support and participation in your community.

6. Collaborate with Influencers and Brands:

Collaborate with other influencers and brands within your niche to amplify your reach and exposure on social media. Partnering with like-minded influencers and brands allows you to tap into their audience and leverage their credibility and influence to grow your own following.

7. Host Giveaways and Contests:

Host giveaways, contests, or challenges to incentivize engagement and attract new followers. Encourage your audience to participate by liking, commenting, sharing, or tagging friends in your posts to enter the giveaway. Promote the giveaway across your social media platforms to maximize participation and reach.

8. Utilize Stories and Live Streams:

Take advantage of stories and live streams to connect with your audience in real-time and create a sense of immediacy and exclusivity. Share behind-the-scenes glimpses, Q&A sessions, product launches, or tutorials through stories and live streams to engage your audience and foster a sense of community.

9. Analyze and Iterate:

Monitor your social media analytics regularly to track your performance, identify trends, and gain insights into what resonates with your audience. Use this data to optimize your content strategy, refine your messaging, and experiment with new approaches to increase followers and engagement.

By implementing these strategies consistently and authentically, you can attract new followers, boost engagement, and build a loyal and engaged community on social media. Stay true to your brand identity, listen to your audience's feedback, and adapt your approach based on their preferences and behaviors to maximize your success as an influencer.

Collaborating with other influencers and brands to expand your reach

Collaborating with other influencers and brands is a powerful strategy for expanding your reach, increasing your visibility, and growing your influence on social media. By partnering with like-minded individuals and reputable brands, you can tap into new audiences, leverage shared credibility, and create mutually beneficial relationships. Here's how to collaborate effectively with other influencers and brands:

1. Identify Compatible Partners:

Start by identifying influencers and brands that share similar values, aesthetics, and target audiences as your own. Look for individuals and companies whose content, messaging, and audience demographics align with your own niche and interests. Collaborating with compatible partners increases the likelihood of a successful partnership and resonates more with your audience.

2. Reach Out and Build Relationships:

Reach out to potential collaborators via email, direct message, or social media to introduce yourself and express your interest in collaborating. Be genuine and personalized in your approach, highlighting what you admire about their work and how you envision a collaboration benefiting both parties. Building genuine relationships with your collaborators fosters trust and rapport, laying the foundation for a successful partnership.

3. Define Clear Objectives and Expectations:

Clearly define the objectives, goals, and expectations for the collaboration upfront to ensure alignment between all parties involved. Determine the scope of the collaboration, desired outcomes, deliverables, and timelines. Establish clear communication channels and roles to facilitate coordination and accountability throughout the collaboration process.

4. Collaborate on Content Creation:

Collaborate with your partners on creating engaging and authentic content that resonates with both audiences. Brainstorm ideas, themes, and concepts together, leveraging each other's strengths and expertise. Co-create content that showcases your unique perspectives, voices, and personalities while aligning with the overarching goals of the collaboration.

5. Cross-Promote Each Other:

Cross-promote each other's content across your respective platforms to maximize exposure and reach. Share each other's posts, stories, and videos with your audience and encourage your followers to follow, engage, and support your collaborators. Tagging and mentioning each other in your posts helps to introduce your audience to your collaborators and vice versa.

6. Host Joint Events or Giveaways:

Host joint events, live streams, or giveaways with your collaborators to create buzz, excitement, and engagement among your audiences. Whether it's a virtual panel discussion, a co-hosted Instagram Live session, or a collaborative giveaway, joint activities encourage participation and interaction from both audiences, driving mutual benefits and exposure.

7. Measure and Evaluate Results:

Track and measure the performance of the collaboration using relevant metrics and analytics tools. Evaluate the impact on key performance indicators such as follower growth, engagement rates, website traffic, and brand sentiment. Gather feedback from your audience and collaborators to assess the success of the collaboration and identify areas for improvement.

8. Nurture Long-Term Relationships:

Cultivate long-term relationships with your collaborators beyond the initial collaboration to foster continued mutual support and collaboration opportunities. Stay in touch, engage with their content, and look for opportunities to collaborate on future projects or initiatives. Nurturing relationships with your collaborators strengthens your network, expands your reach, and opens doors to new opportunities in the future.

By collaborating strategically with other influencers and brands, you can amplify your reach, increase your visibility, and create meaningful connections with new audiences. Stay open-minded, be proactive in reaching out to potential collaborators, and approach collaborations with authenticity, creativity, and professionalism to maximize the benefits for all parties involved.

Chapter 6: Monetizing Your Influence

Exploring different revenue streams for influencers (e.g., sponsored content, affiliate marketing, product sales)

Exploring different revenue streams is essential for influencers looking to diversify their income and monetize their influence effectively. While sponsored content is a common revenue stream for influencers, there are various other opportunities to generate income and create sustainable revenue streams. Here are some popular revenue streams for influencers:

1. Sponsored Content:

Sponsored content involves collaborating with brands to create content that promotes their products or services in exchange for compensation. Influencers can work with brands on sponsored posts, videos, stories, or live streams, providing exposure to a brand's target audience and driving engagement and conversions.

2. Affiliate Marketing:

Affiliate marketing allows influencers to earn a commission for promoting products or services and driving sales through tracked affiliate links. Influencers can partner with affiliate networks, individual brands, or e-commerce platforms to promote products they genuinely recommend to their audience. When followers make a purchase through the influencer's affiliate link, the influencer earns a commission on the sale.

3. Product Sales:

Influencers can create and sell their own products or merchandise to their audience, leveraging their personal brand and influence to drive sales. This can include digital products such as e-books, online courses, presets, or templates, as well as physical products such as branded merchandise, clothing, or accessories. Selling products directly to your audience allows influencers to retain control over pricing, branding, and customer relationships.

4. Brand Partnerships and Ambassadorships:

In addition to sponsored content, influencers can establish long-term partnerships or ambassadorships with brands to represent them on an ongoing basis. Brand partnerships may involve co-creating products, serving as brand ambassadors, or participating in exclusive events and campaigns. Long-term collaborations provide influencers with consistent income and opportunities for deeper engagement with brands and their audience.

5. Content Licensing and Syndication:

Influencers can monetize their content by licensing it to media outlets, brands, or other content creators for use in advertising, marketing campaigns, or editorial purposes. This can include licensing photos, videos, articles, or other original content for a fee, providing influencers with additional revenue streams and exposure opportunities.

6. Sponsored Events and Experiences:

Influencers can host sponsored events, workshops, or experiences in collaboration with brands, sponsors, or event organizers. Sponsored events provide influencers with opportunities to engage with their audience in person, showcase products or services, and create memorable experiences that drive brand awareness and affinity.

7. Digital Advertising and Sponsorships:

Influencers can monetize their digital platforms, such as blogs, websites, or podcasts, through display advertising, sponsored content placements, or sponsored newsletters. By partnering with advertising networks, brands, or sponsors, influencers can generate revenue from ad impressions, clicks, or sponsorships on their digital properties.

8. Consulting and Coaching Services:

Influencers can leverage their expertise, knowledge, and experience to offer consulting, coaching, or mentoring services to other influencers, brands, or businesses. This can include providing guidance on content creation, social media strategy, brand development, or influencer marketing, charging fees for one-on-one consultations, workshops, or group coaching programs.

By exploring and diversifying their revenue streams, influencers can create multiple income streams, reduce dependency on any single source of income, and build a more sustainable and profitable influencer business. It's important for influencers to evaluate their skills, interests, and audience preferences when exploring different revenue opportunities and to prioritize partnerships and opportunities that align with their personal brand and values.

Negotiating deals with brands and advertisers

Negotiating deals with brands and advertisers is a crucial skill for influencers looking to secure profitable partnerships and collaborations. Effective negotiation can help influencers maximize their earning potential, protect their interests, and build mutually beneficial relationships with brands. Here are some tips for negotiating deals with brands and advertisers:

1. Know Your Worth:

   Before entering into negotiations, have a clear understanding of your value as an influencer. Consider factors such as your audience size, engagement rates, content quality, niche expertise, and past performance in similar collaborations. Use this information to establish a baseline for your rates and negotiate from a position of confidence and professionalism.

2. Research the Brand:

Familiarize yourself with the brand's products, services, target audience, and marketing objectives before entering into negotiations. Research the brand's past collaborations with influencers, their budget allocations for influencer marketing, and their overall approach to partnerships. Tailor your pitch and negotiation strategy to align with the brand's goals and preferences.

3. Define Your Terms and Expectations:

Clearly define your terms, expectations, and deliverables upfront to avoid misunderstandings or misalignments later on. Outline key details such as the scope of work, content format and specifications, posting schedule, usage rights, compensation structure, and payment terms. Be specific and transparent about what you can offer and what you expect in return from the brand.

4. Showcase Your Value Proposition:

Highlight the unique value proposition you bring to the table as an influencer. Emphasize your audience demographics, engagement metrics, brand affinity, storytelling abilities, and ability to drive results for the brand. Showcase examples of past successful collaborations, case studies, testimonials, or metrics that demonstrate your impact and effectiveness as an influencer.

5. Negotiate from a Win-Win Perspective:

Approach negotiations with a mindset of collaboration and mutual benefit. Seek to understand the brand's objectives, challenges, and constraints, and look for creative ways to address their needs while also achieving your own goals. Focus on building a long-term partnership based on trust, respect, and shared value rather than maximizing short-term gains.

6. Be Flexible and Open to Compromise:

Be flexible and open to compromise during negotiations to reach a mutually satisfactory agreement with the brand. Consider alternative compensation structures, value-added benefits, or performance-based incentives that align with both parties' interests. Be willing to negotiate on certain terms while standing firm on others that are non-negotiable for you.

7. Document the Agreement:

Once you've reached an agreement with the brand, document the terms and conditions of the collaboration in a formal contract or agreement. Clearly outline all the agreed-upon terms, deliverables, timelines, and payment details to ensure clarity and accountability on both sides.

Review the contract carefully before signing and seek legal advice if needed.

8. Maintain Professionalism and Communication:

Throughout the negotiation process, maintain professionalism, transparency, and open communication with the brand or advertiser. Respond promptly to inquiries, address any concerns or questions, and keep the brand informed of any changes or updates related to the collaboration. Building a positive rapport and fostering trust with the brand can lead to future opportunities for collaboration.

By mastering the art of negotiation and approaching brand deals with confidence, professionalism, and a collaborative mindset, influencers can secure lucrative partnerships, build valuable relationships with brands, and unlock new opportunities for growth and success in their influencer careers.

Building long-term partnerships and sustainable income streams

Building long-term partnerships and sustainable income streams is essential for influencers looking to establish a successful and profitable influencer career. While one-off collaborations and short-term sponsorships can provide immediate income, long-term partnerships offer stability, consistency, and growth opportunities. Here's how influencers can build long-term partnerships and sustainable income streams:

1. Establish Trust and Credibility:

Focus on building trust and credibility with brands and advertisers by consistently delivering high-quality content, meeting deadlines, and exceeding expectations. Demonstrate your professionalism, reliability, and commitment to excellence in every collaboration. By establishing yourself as a trusted and reputable influencer, brands will be more inclined to partner with you on a long-term basis.

2. Showcase Your Value:

Highlight the unique value you bring to brands as an influencer, emphasizing your audience demographics, engagement metrics, content quality, and ability to drive results. Showcase examples of past successful collaborations, case studies, testimonials, or performance metrics that demonstrate your impact and effectiveness as a partner. By clearly articulating your value proposition, you'll attract brands seeking long-term partnerships with influencers who can deliver tangible results.

3. Align with Brand Values and Objectives:

Seek out brands that align with your values, interests, and niche expertise, and whose products or services resonate with your audience. Look for brands with long-term marketing objectives and a commitment to building authentic and meaningful relationships with influencers. By aligning with brands that share your values and objectives, you'll establish a strong foundation for a successful and sustainable partnership.

4. Foster Open Communication:

Maintain open and transparent communication with brands throughout the partnership, keeping them informed of your progress, performance, and any relevant updates or changes. Seek feedback from brands on your content and collaboration process, and be receptive to constructive criticism or suggestions for improvement. By fostering clear and effective communication, you'll strengthen your relationship with brands and ensure alignment on expectations and goals.

5. Provide Value Beyond Sponsored Content:

Offer value to brands beyond sponsored content by providing insights, feedback, and strategic input on their products, marketing campaigns, or brand initiatives. Share your audience's feedback, preferences, and insights with brands to help them refine their messaging, improve their products, or optimize their marketing strategies. By demonstrating your expertise and adding value beyond sponsored content, you'll position yourself as a valuable partner for long-term collaboration.

6. Diversify Your Revenue Streams:

Explore and leverage multiple revenue streams beyond sponsored content to create a more sustainable income as an influencer. This can include affiliate marketing, product sales, digital products, brand ambassadorships, consulting services, or sponsored events. Diversifying your revenue streams reduces dependency on any single source of income and provides stability and resilience in the face of fluctuations in the influencer market.

7. Nurture Relationships with Brands:

Cultivate long-term relationships with brands by nurturing trust, loyalty, and mutual respect over time. Stay in touch with brand contacts, engage with their content, and look for opportunities to support and promote their brand organically. Invest time and effort in building genuine connections with brand representatives, fostering a positive rapport, and staying top-of-mind for future collaboration opportunities.

8. Adapt and Evolve:

Stay adaptable and responsive to changes in the influencer landscape, industry trends, and brand preferences. Continuously refine your content strategy, audience engagement tactics, and partnership approach based on feedback, insights, and emerging opportunities. By staying agile and evolving with the industry, you'll remain relevant and competitive in the influencer market and continue to attract long-term partnerships and sustainable income streams.

By focusing on building long-term partnerships with brands, providing value beyond sponsored content, and diversifying their revenue streams, influencers can create a sustainable and profitable influencer career that withstands the test of time and delivers consistent income and growth opportunities in the long run.

Chapter 7: Managing Your Online Presence

Dealing with trolls, negativity, and criticism

Dealing with trolls, negativity, and criticism is an inevitable part of being an influencer, but it's essential to develop effective strategies for managing and mitigating the impact of negative feedback on your mental health and well-being. Here are some tips for handling trolls, negativity, and criticism as an influencer:

1. Develop Thick Skin:

Recognize that receiving negative comments and criticism is a common experience for influencers and public figures. Develop resilience and cultivate a mindset that enables you to withstand criticism without taking it personally. Remind yourself that negative feedback often says more about the commenter than it does about you.

2. Don't Engage with Trolls:

Avoid engaging with trolls or responding to negative comments that are intended to provoke or instigate conflict. Engaging with trolls only fuels their behavior and gives them the attention they crave. Instead, focus your energy on creating positive content and interacting with genuine followers who appreciate and support your work.

3. Set Boundaries:

Establish clear boundaries for what type of behavior and language you will tolerate on your social media platforms. Create community guidelines or moderation policies that outline acceptable conduct and consequences for violating those guidelines. Enforce your boundaries consistently and impartially to maintain a safe and respectful online environment for your audience.

4. Use Moderation Tools:

Take advantage of moderation tools and features available on social media platforms to manage negative comments and block or mute abusive users. Use keyword filters, comment moderation settings, and user blocking features to filter out inappropriate or offensive content and protect yourself from harassment and abuse.

5. Focus on the Positive:

Shift your focus away from negative comments and criticism and concentrate on the positive feedback and support you receive from genuine followers. Surround yourself with positivity by engaging with supportive comments, messages, and interactions from your audience. Celebrate your achievements and milestones, and remind yourself of the positive impact you're making on your audience.

6. Practice Self-Care:

Prioritize self-care and well-being to maintain your mental and emotional health in the face of negativity and criticism. Practice mindfulness, meditation, or relaxation techniques to manage stress and anxiety. Take breaks from social media when needed to recharge and disconnect from negativity. Surround yourself with supportive friends, family, and colleagues who uplift and encourage you.

7. Seek Support:

Reach out to trusted friends, family members, or fellow influencers for support and encouragement during challenging times. Share your experiences and feelings with others who understand the pressures and realities of being an influencer. Consider joining online communities or support groups for influencers to connect with like-minded individuals and share advice and resources.

8. Learn and Grow:

Use negative feedback and criticism as an opportunity for learning and growth. Reflect on constructive criticism and consider whether there are areas where you can improve or evolve as an influencer. Use feedback as a catalyst for self-improvement and professional development, but also recognize when criticism is unfounded or unhelpful and learn to let it go.

By adopting these strategies for dealing with trolls, negativity, and criticism, influencers can protect their mental health and well-being, maintain a positive and supportive online community, and continue to create meaningful content that resonates with their audience. Remember that you're not alone in facing negativity as an influencer, and it's okay to seek help and support when needed.

Maintaining authenticity and transparency with your audience

Maintaining authenticity and transparency with your audience is crucial for building trust, credibility, and long-term relationships as an influencer. Authenticity involves being genuine, honest, and true to yourself, while transparency entails being open, clear, and upfront with your audience about your intentions, affiliations, and experiences. Here are some strategies for maintaining authenticity and transparency with your audience:

1. Be True to Yourself:

Stay true to your values, beliefs, and personality in everything you do as an influencer. Avoid pretending to be someone you're not or adopting a persona that doesn't align with your authentic self. Authenticity shines through when you share your genuine passions, interests, and experiences with your audience, allowing them to connect with you on a deeper level.

2. Share Your Story:

Share personal anecdotes, experiences, and insights with your audience to humanize your brand and create a sense of authenticity. Be open and vulnerable about your successes, failures, challenges, and lessons learned along your journey as an influencer. Sharing your story helps your audience relate to you on a personal level and fosters a stronger emotional connection.

3. Disclose Partnerships and Sponsored Content:

Be transparent with your audience about any partnerships, sponsorships, or paid promotions you participate in. Clearly disclose your affiliations and relationships with brands in your content, captions, or disclosures to maintain transparency and trust with your audience. Use hashtags such as #ad, #sponsored, or #partner to indicate sponsored content and ensure compliance with advertising guidelines.

4. Avoid Misleading or Deceptive Practices:

Refrain from engaging in misleading or deceptive practices that undermine your authenticity and credibility as an influencer. Be honest and transparent about your experiences, opinions, and recommendations, and avoid exaggerating or misrepresenting information to your audience. Prioritize integrity and honesty in all your interactions and communications.

5. Engage Authentically with Your Audience:

Foster genuine and meaningful interactions with your audience by responding to comments, messages, and mentions authentically. Show appreciation for your followers' support and feedback, and engage in two-way conversations that demonstrate your genuine interest and respect for your audience. Avoid generic or automated responses and strive to connect with your audience on a personal level.

6. Admit Mistakes and Take Accountability:

Be willing to admit mistakes, take accountability for your actions, and apologize when necessary. Nobody is perfect, and acknowledging your imperfections and shortcomings demonstrates humility and authenticity to your audience. Use mistakes as learning opportunities and strive to do better in the future, maintaining transparency and integrity in the process.

7. Be Consistent and Reliable:

Consistency is key to maintaining authenticity and trust with your audience. Stay consistent in your messaging, content quality, and engagement efforts across all your platforms and channels. Be reliable and dependable in delivering on your promises, commitments, and obligations to your audience and brand partners.

8. Seek Feedback and Listen to Your Audience:

Actively seek feedback from your audience and listen to their opinions, suggestions, and concerns. Encourage open dialogue and constructive criticism, and be receptive to feedback that helps you improve and grow as an influencer. By listening to your audience and incorporating their feedback into your content and approach, you demonstrate your commitment to their needs and preferences.

By prioritizing authenticity and transparency in your interactions and communications with your audience, you can build a loyal and engaged community of followers who trust and respect you as an influencer. Authenticity and transparency are not only ethical principles but also essential ingredients for long-term success and impact as an influencer in a competitive and ever-evolving digital landscape.

Balancing personal and professional boundaries

Balancing personal and professional boundaries is essential for maintaining your well-being, authenticity, and professionalism as an influencer. As you navigate your influencer career, it's important to establish clear boundaries between your personal life and your public persona, ensuring that you protect your privacy, mental health, and personal relationships. Here are some strategies for effectively balancing personal and professional boundaries as an influencer:

1. Define Your Boundaries:

Take time to reflect on your personal values, priorities, and boundaries, both online and offline. Identify areas where you're comfortable sharing and areas where you prefer to keep private. Consider factors such as your family, relationships, health, finances, and mental well-being when setting boundaries for your influencer career.

2. Establish Clear Guidelines:

Establish clear guidelines and boundaries for yourself in terms of the content you create, the information you share, and the interactions you have with your audience. Define what topics, experiences, and aspects of your personal life are off-limits for public consumption and stick to those boundaries consistently.

3. Communicate Boundaries Effectively:

Communicate your boundaries effectively with your audience, brand partners, and collaborators to ensure mutual understanding and respect. Use your bio, about page, or FAQ section to outline your boundaries and preferences for engagement, collaboration, and content creation. Be firm yet polite in enforcing your boundaries and addressing any violations respectfully.

4. Prioritize Self-Care:

Prioritize self-care and well-being to maintain a healthy balance between your personal and professional life. Set aside dedicated time for rest, relaxation, hobbies, and activities that nourish your mind, body, and soul. Create boundaries around your work hours, social media use, and digital consumption to prevent burnout and maintain a sense of balance.

5. Limit Accessibility:

Limit accessibility and availability to maintain boundaries between your personal and professional life. Set specific times for engaging with your audience, responding to messages, and creating content, and avoid being constantly available or responsive around the clock. Establish digital detox periods or tech-free zones to disconnect from social media and recharge offline.

6. Respect Privacy:

Respect the privacy and consent of yourself and others when sharing content or engaging with your audience online. Avoid oversharing personal details or sensitive information that could compromise your safety, security, or well-being. Obtain explicit consent from friends, family members, or individuals featured in your content before sharing their images, stories, or experiences publicly.

7. Seek Support and Guidance:

Seek support and guidance from trusted friends, family members, or mentors when navigating personal and professional boundaries as an influencer. Surround yourself with people who understand and respect your boundaries and can provide perspective, advice, and encouragement when needed.

8. Regularly Reevaluate and Adjust:

Regularly reevaluate your boundaries and adjust them as needed based on changes in your life, career, or circumstances. Be flexible and open-minded in reassessing your boundaries and adapting them to reflect your evolving needs, priorities, and goals as an influencer.

By establishing clear boundaries, prioritizing self-care, and communicating effectively with your audience and collaborators, you can maintain a healthy balance between your personal and professional life as an influencer. Striking the right balance allows you to protect your privacy, well-being, and personal relationships while also thriving in your influencer career with authenticity, integrity, and professionalism.

Chapter 8: Evolving as an Influencer

Staying relevant in a constantly changing digital landscape

Staying relevant in a constantly changing digital landscape is essential for influencers looking to maintain visibility, engagement, and growth in their careers. As trends, algorithms, and audience preferences evolve, influencers must adapt and innovate to remain competitive and impactful in the ever-changing online world. Here are some strategies for staying relevant as an influencer:

1. Stay Informed and Educated:

Stay up-to-date with the latest trends, news, and developments in the digital and social media landscape. Follow industry blogs, newsletters, podcasts, and publications to stay informed about emerging platforms, features, and best practices. Attend conferences, webinars, or workshops to expand your knowledge and skills in areas relevant to your niche.

2. Monitor Audience Preferences:

Keep a close eye on your audience's preferences, behaviors, and engagement patterns to identify emerging trends and opportunities. Monitor metrics such as engagement rates, click-through rates, and audience demographics to understand what content resonates most with your audience. Use insights from analytics tools and audience feedback to tailor your content strategy and stay relevant to your audience's interests.

3. Experiment with New Formats and Platforms:

Experiment with new content formats, platforms, and features to diversify your content and reach new audiences. Stay open-minded and willing to explore emerging platforms such as TikTok, Clubhouse, or Twitch, as well as new features like Reels, Stories, or Live Streams on existing platforms. Adapt your content strategy to take advantage of new opportunities and stay ahead of the curve.

4. Collaborate and Network:

Collaborate with other influencers, creators, and brands to expand your reach, exposure, and relevance in the digital landscape. Partnering with like-minded individuals and reputable brands allows you to tap into new audiences, leverage shared credibility, and create mutually beneficial relationships. Collaborate on joint projects, campaigns, or events to amplify your impact and stay top-of-mind for your audience.

5. Innovate and Be Creative:

Embrace innovation and creativity in your content creation process to differentiate yourself and stand out in a crowded digital landscape. Experiment with unique ideas, formats, and concepts that showcase your creativity and captivate your audience's attention. Stay true to your brand identity while pushing the boundaries and exploring new ways to engage and inspire your audience.

6. Engage Authentically with Your Audience:

Foster genuine and meaningful interactions with your audience by engaging authentically with their comments, messages, and feedback. Be responsive, approachable, and transparent in your communications, and show appreciation for your followers' support and participation. Build a loyal and engaged community by prioritizing connection and conversation with your audience.

7. Adapt to Algorithm Changes:

Stay informed about algorithm changes and updates on social media platforms and adjust your content strategy accordingly. Keep an eye on platform-specific best practices, guidelines, and recommendations to optimize your content for maximum visibility and engagement. Experiment with different posting times, frequencies, and content formats to adapt to algorithmic changes and maintain your relevance on social media.

8. Evolve with Your Audience:

Evolve and grow alongside your audience by listening to their feedback, preferences, and needs. Pay attention to shifts in demographics, interests, and behaviors within your audience and adjust your content strategy accordingly. Stay relevant by addressing relevant topics, challenges, and trends that resonate with your audience's evolving interests and aspirations.

By staying informed, adaptable, and innovative, influencers can navigate the constantly changing digital landscape with confidence and relevance. Embrace change as an opportunity for growth and evolution, and continue to engage, inspire, and connect with your audience authentically in the ever-evolving world of digital media.

Adapting to new social media trends and platforms

Adapting to new social media trends and platforms is essential for influencers seeking to maintain relevance, visibility, and engagement in an ever-evolving digital landscape. As new platforms emerge and existing ones introduce new features and functionalities, influencers must stay agile and proactive in embracing these changes to reach and connect with their audience effectively. Here are some strategies for adapting to new social media trends and platforms:

1. Stay Informed and Curious:

Stay curious and open-minded about emerging social media trends, platforms, and features. Follow industry news, blogs, and publications to stay informed about the latest developments and innovations in the digital landscape. Keep an eye on emerging platforms and trends that are gaining traction among your target audience.

2. Experiment and Explore:

Don't be afraid to experiment with new social media platforms, features, and formats to see what resonates with your audience. Set aside time for exploration and experimentation to familiarize yourself with new platforms such as TikTok, Clubhouse, or Reels, and experiment with different content formats, styles, and strategies to gauge audience response.

3. Observe and Learn from Others:

Observe how other influencers, creators, and brands are leveraging new social media trends and platforms to engage their audience effectively. Pay attention to what types of content perform well, how audiences interact with new features, and what strategies are driving engagement and growth. Learn from their successes and failures to inform your own approach.

4. Adapt Your Content Strategy:

Adapt your content strategy to align with the unique characteristics and audience preferences of each social media platform. Tailor your content format, tone, and messaging to fit the platform's format and audience demographics. Experiment with different content types, such as short-form videos, live streams, or interactive polls, to engage your audience in new and exciting ways.

5. Optimize for Platform-Specific Features:

Take advantage of platform-specific features and functionalities to enhance the visibility and engagement of your content. Stay informed about new features and updates introduced by social media platforms and incorporate them into your content strategy. Use features such as hashtags, stickers, filters, and interactive elements to make your content more discoverable and engaging.

6. Engage with Your Audience:

Foster genuine and meaningful interactions with your audience across all social media platforms. Respond to comments, messages, and mentions promptly, and actively engage with your audience through likes, shares, and replies. Encourage conversation and feedback from your audience to build a strong sense of community and connection.

7. Monitor Performance and Iterate:

Monitor the performance of your content on new social media platforms and iterate your approach based on audience feedback and analytics. Track metrics such as reach, engagement, and follower growth to gauge the effectiveness of your content strategy. Experiment with different tactics, analyze the results, and adjust your strategy accordingly to optimize your performance over time.

8. Stay Flexible and Adapt Quickly:

Stay flexible and adaptable in responding to changes and trends in the social media landscape. Be willing to pivot your strategy or experiment with new approaches based on evolving audience preferences, platform updates, or competitive dynamics. Stay nimble and proactive in adapting to new trends and platforms to stay ahead of the curve and maintain your relevance as an influencer.

By staying informed, curious, and adaptable, influencers can effectively navigate the ever-changing social media landscape and leverage new trends and platforms to reach and engage their audience in meaningful ways. Embrace change as an opportunity for growth and innovation, and continue to evolve your content strategy to meet the evolving needs and preferences of your audience.

Continuing education and professional development

Continuing education and professional development are crucial for influencers aiming to thrive and stay relevant in the dynamic landscape of digital media. Whether you're an established influencer or just starting out, dedicating time and effort to ongoing learning is essential for honing your skills, expanding your knowledge, and adapting to industry trends. Here's why continuing education matters for influencers and how to approach it effectively:

Why Continuing Education Matters:

1. Adaptability: The digital landscape is constantly evolving, with new platforms, trends, and algorithms emerging regularly. Continuing education helps influencers stay adaptable and responsive to these changes, ensuring they can pivot their strategies and stay ahead of the curve.

2. Skill Enhancement: Professional development opportunities allow influencers to enhance their skills in areas such as content creation, social media management, branding, analytics, and more. Developing these skills not only improves the quality of your content but also increases your value to brands and collaborators.

3. Industry Knowledge: Keeping up with industry news, trends, and best practices is essential for influencers looking to maintain their relevance and credibility. Continuous learning allows influencers to stay informed about the latest developments in influencer marketing, platform updates, and audience behaviors.

4. Networking Opportunities: Engaging in educational events, workshops, and courses provides opportunities to network

with other influencers, industry experts, and brands. Building these connections can lead to collaboration opportunities, mentorship, and valuable insights that can further your career as an influencer.

Strategies for Continuing Education:

1. Attend Workshops and Webinars: Look for workshops, webinars, and online courses that cover topics relevant to your niche and interests. Many platforms offer free or paid educational resources on content creation, social media strategy, branding, and more. Participating in these sessions can provide valuable insights and practical skills to apply to your influencer career.

2. Join Professional Communities: Join online communities, forums, or social media groups specifically tailored to influencers. These communities often provide opportunities for networking, knowledge sharing, and collaboration. Engage with other members, ask questions, and contribute to discussions to make the most of these communities.

3. Seek Mentorship: Consider seeking mentorship from experienced influencers or industry professionals who can provide guidance and advice based on their own experiences. A mentor can offer valuable insights, help you navigate challenges, and provide support as you grow your influencer career.

4. Read Industry Publications: Stay informed about industry trends, news, and insights by regularly reading industry publications, blogs, newsletters, and podcasts. Subscribe to relevant publications and set aside time each week to catch up on the latest developments in the influencer marketing space.

5. Experiment and Learn by Doing: One of the best ways to learn as an influencer is through hands-on experimentation. Don't be afraid to try new content formats, strategies, or platforms, and use analytics to evaluate their effectiveness. Learning from your own successes and failures can be a powerful way to refine your approach and improve over time.

6. Set Learning Goals: Set specific learning goals for yourself to guide your professional development efforts. Identify areas where you'd like to improve or learn new skills, and create a plan for achieving those goals. Whether it's mastering a new editing technique or understanding the intricacies of a social media algorithm, having clear goals can help you stay focused and motivated.

7. Stay Curious and Open-Minded: Finally, approach continuing education with a mindset of curiosity and openness. The digital landscape is constantly evolving, and there's always something new to learn. Stay curious about emerging trends, platforms, and technologies, and be open to exploring new ideas and approaches that can help you grow as an influencer.

Continuing education and professional development are ongoing processes that require dedication and commitment. By investing in your own learning and growth as an influencer, you can stay competitive, adapt to industry changes, and build a successful and sustainable career in the ever-evolving world of digital media.

Chapter 9: Case Studies and Success Stories

Interviews with successful influencers in various niches

Interviews with successful influencers in various niches provide valuable insights, inspiration, and practical advice for aspiring influencers looking to grow their own brands and audiences. By learning from the experiences, strategies, and perspectives of established influencers, aspiring creators can gain valuable knowledge and guidance to help them navigate the competitive landscape of influencer marketing. Here's how interviews with successful influencers in various niches can benefit aspiring creators:

Insights into Niche Expertise:

1. In-Depth Knowledge: Successful influencers have deep expertise in their respective niches, whether it's fashion, beauty, fitness, gaming, or travel. Interviews with these influencers provide insights into the nuances of their niche, including current trends, audience preferences, and industry dynamics.

2. Tactical Strategies: Influencers often share practical strategies and tactics they've used to grow their audience, engage their followers, and monetize their content. Interviews provide a platform for influencers to discuss their content creation process, social media strategy, collaboration approach, and other actionable tips for success.

Personal Journey and Brand Building:

1. Origin Stories: Learning about an influencer's journey from aspiring creator to successful brand can be both inspiring and informative. Interviews often delve into an influencer's backstory, including their motivations, challenges, and pivotal moments along the way.

2. Brand Identity: Successful influencers have a clear brand identity that resonates with their audience and sets them apart from competitors. Interviews explore how influencers have developed their brand identity, including their aesthetic, messaging, values, and unique selling proposition.

Engagement and Community Building:

1. Audience Engagement: Interviews with successful influencers shed light on how they've built and nurtured a loyal and engaged audience over time. From responding to comments and messages to hosting live Q&A sessions,

influencers share their strategies for fostering meaningful connections with their followers.

2. Community Building: Influencers often discuss how they've cultivated a sense of community among their followers, creating a supportive and inclusive space for like-minded individuals to connect and engage. Interviews explore the role of community building in an influencer's success and the impact it has on audience loyalty and brand advocacy.

Monetization and Business Strategies:

1. Diversified Revenue Streams: Successful influencers have diversified revenue streams beyond brand sponsorships, including affiliate marketing, product sales, sponsored content, and more. Interviews provide insights into how influencers monetize their platforms and the strategies they use to generate income.

2. Negotiation and Collaboration: Influencers share their experiences negotiating deals with brands and collaborating with other creators, agencies, and industry partners. Interviews offer insights into the negotiation process, including setting rates, defining deliverables, and establishing mutually beneficial partnerships.

Adaptation to Industry Changes:

1. Adaptability: The influencer landscape is constantly evolving, with new platforms, algorithms, and trends shaping the industry. Interviews with successful influencers highlight their ability to adapt to these changes, pivot their strategies, and stay ahead of the curve.

2. Lessons Learned: Influencers often reflect on their successes and failures, sharing valuable lessons learned along the way. Interviews provide a platform for influencers to impart wisdom, advice, and cautionary tales to aspiring creators, helping them avoid common pitfalls and navigate the challenges of the influencer industry.

Overall, interviews with successful influencers in various niches offer a wealth of knowledge, inspiration, and practical advice for aspiring creators looking to build their own brands and audiences. By learning from the experiences and strategies of those who have achieved success in the influencer space, aspiring creators can gain valuable insights to inform their own journey and increase their chances of success.

Analyzing their strategies and key takeaways

Analyzing the strategies and key takeaways from interviews with successful influencers provides valuable insights into what it takes to build a thriving presence in the digital landscape. By dissecting the approaches, tactics, and mindset of these influencers, aspiring creators can glean actionable lessons and apply them to their own journey. Here's how to analyze their strategies and distill key takeaways:

Identify Core Strategies:

1. Content Creation: Examine how successful influencers approach content creation, including their creative process, content formats, and themes. Analyze the types of content that resonate most with their audience and how they maintain consistency and quality over time.

2. Audience Engagement: Explore the strategies successful influencers use to engage their audience, including responding to comments, hosting Q&A sessions, and fostering community interaction. Look for patterns in how they build rapport and foster a sense of connection with their followers.

3. Platform Utilization: Assess how influencers leverage different social media platforms and features to maximize their reach and engagement. Identify which platforms are most effective for their niche and audience demographic and how they adapt their content for each platform.

Extract Key Takeaways:

1. Authenticity: One common theme among successful influencers is authenticity. Take note of how influencers stay true to their voice, values, and interests, and how authenticity contributes to audience trust and loyalty.

2. Consistency: Consistency is key to maintaining visibility and engagement as an influencer. Pay attention to how successful influencers maintain a consistent posting schedule, aesthetic, and messaging across their platforms.

3. Community Building: Successful influencers prioritize community building as a means of fostering a loyal and engaged audience. Learn how they cultivate a sense of belonging among their followers and encourage active participation in their content.

Evaluate Monetization Strategies:

1. Diversification: Assess the various revenue streams successful influencers utilize beyond brand sponsorships, including affiliate marketing, product sales, memberships, and more. Identify opportunities to diversify your own income streams to reduce reliance on any single source.

2. Negotiation Skills: Learn from successful influencers' experiences in negotiating deals with brands and collaborators. Pay attention to how they establish fair rates,

define deliverables, and maintain positive long-term relationships with partners.

Adaptability and Growth:

1. Adaptation: Successful influencers demonstrate adaptability in response to changes in the digital landscape. Analyze how they stay ahead of trends, pivot their strategies, and leverage new opportunities to sustain growth and relevance.

2. Continuous Learning: Note the emphasis successful influencers place on continuous learning and professional development. Identify opportunities to expand your skills, knowledge, and expertise to remain competitive in the ever-evolving influencer industry.

Implementation and Experimentation:

1. Actionable Insights: Extract actionable insights from successful influencers' strategies and apply them to your own content creation, engagement, and monetization efforts. Experiment with new tactics and approaches to see what works best for your unique audience and niche.

2. Iterative Process: Recognize that success as an influencer is often an iterative process of experimentation, analysis,

and refinement. Be willing to adapt and evolve your strategies based on feedback, data, and changing market conditions.

By carefully analyzing the strategies and key takeaways from interviews with successful influencers, aspiring creators can gain valuable insights into the principles, tactics, and mindset that contribute to influencer success. Apply these lessons thoughtfully to your own journey, and continuously iterate and refine your approach as you strive to build a thriving presence in the digital landscape.

Inspiration and insights for aspiring influencers

For aspiring influencers, seeking inspiration and insights from successful creators is an invaluable resource on their journey to establishing a thriving presence in the digital world. Learning from the experiences, strategies, and challenges of those who have already achieved success can provide aspiring influencers with valuable guidance, motivation, and direction. Here's how inspiration and insights from successful influencers can benefit those just starting out:

Motivation and Encouragement:

1. Proof of Possibility: Seeing others achieve success as influencers serves as tangible proof that it's possible to turn

a passion into a profession. Aspiring influencers can draw motivation and encouragement from the stories of those who have overcome obstacles and achieved their goals in the influencer space.

2. Role Models: Successful influencers often serve as role models for aspiring creators, demonstrating what's possible with hard work, dedication, and creativity. By studying the journeys of these role models, aspiring influencers can gain valuable inspiration and a roadmap for their own path forward.

Learning from Experience:

1. Practical Insights: Interviews and case studies with successful influencers provide practical insights into the strategies, tactics, and mindset that contribute to influencer success. Aspiring influencers can learn from the experiences, successes, and failures of those who have navigated the challenges of building a brand and audience online.

2. Key Takeaways: Analyzing the strategies and key takeaways from successful influencers helps aspiring creators distill actionable lessons that they can apply to their own journey. Whether it's tips for content creation, audience engagement, or monetization, there's a wealth of knowledge to be gained from studying the approaches of those who have come before.

Navigating Challenges:

1. Overcoming Obstacles: Successful influencers often share stories of the challenges they've faced along the way, from content creation hurdles to brand partnerships and algorithm changes. By learning how others have overcome these obstacles, aspiring influencers can better prepare themselves for the road ahead and navigate challenges more effectively.

2. Resilience and Persistence: Learning about the persistence and resilience of successful influencers can inspire aspiring creators to persevere in the face of setbacks and setbacks. By understanding that success often requires dedication, hard work, and resilience, aspiring influencers can approach their journey with a mindset of perseverance and determination.

Building Confidence and Identity:

1. Finding Your Voice: Seeing others succeed as influencers can help aspiring creators find the confidence to embrace their own unique voice, style, and identity. By studying the diverse range of creators who have found success online, aspiring influencers can gain the courage to be authentic and true to themselves in their content.

2. Embracing Uniqueness: Successful influencers often emphasize the importance of authenticity and originality in standing out online. By celebrating their own unique interests, perspectives, and talents, aspiring influencers can carve out their own niche and attract an audience who resonates with their authentic self.

Fostering Community:

1. Connecting with Peers: Engaging with the influencer community allows aspiring creators to connect with peers who share similar aspirations and challenges. By participating in online communities, forums, and social media groups, aspiring influencers can find support, advice, and camaraderie from others on the same journey.

2. Collaboration Opportunities: Learning from successful influencers can open doors to collaboration opportunities and mentorship relationships. By reaching out to established creators for advice or collaboration, aspiring influencers can build valuable connections and learn from those who have walked the path before them.

In summary, inspiration and insights from successful influencers provide aspiring creators with motivation, guidance, and encouragement on their journey to becoming influential voices in the digital world. By learning from the experiences, strategies, and challenges of those who have achieved success, aspiring influencers can gain valuable knowledge, confidence, and direction to pursue their own dreams and aspirations in the influencer space.

Chapter 10: The Future of Influence

Predictions for the future of influencer marketing

Predicting the future of influencer marketing requires a deep understanding of current trends, technological advancements, and shifts in consumer behavior. While it's impossible to predict with absolute certainty, several key trends and developments suggest where influencer marketing might be headed in the coming years. Here are some predictions for the future of influencer marketing:

Rise of Micro-Influencers:

1. Authenticity and Engagement: As consumers become increasingly savvy and discerning, the demand for authenticity and genuine connections will continue to grow. Micro-influencers, who often have smaller but highly engaged and loyal followings, will play a crucial role in delivering authentic and relatable content to niche audiences.

2. Hyper-Targeted Campaigns: Brands will increasingly turn to micro-influencers to reach specific demographics and niche markets. By collaborating with influencers who have a deep understanding of their audience's interests and preferences, brands can create hyper-targeted campaigns that resonate more effectively with their target customers.

Emphasis on Long-Term Relationships:

1. Building Trust and Credibility: Brands will prioritize building long-term relationships with influencers to foster trust and credibility with their audience. Rather than one-off partnerships, brands will seek to establish ongoing collaborations with influencers who align with their values and brand identity.

2. Ambassador Programs: Ambassador programs, where influencers have an ongoing relationship with a brand over an extended period, will become more prevalent. These programs allow influencers to become genuine advocates for a brand, creating authentic and consistent content that resonates with their audience over time.

Integration of New Technologies:

1. Augmented Reality (AR) and Virtual Reality (VR): The integration of AR and VR technologies into influencer marketing will offer new opportunities for immersive and

interactive content experiences. Influencers will leverage AR filters, virtual try-on experiences, and immersive storytelling to engage their audience in innovative ways.

2. AI-Powered Content Creation: AI-powered tools and platforms will empower influencers to create more personalized, data-driven content at scale. From content ideation and creation to audience segmentation and optimization, AI will streamline the content creation process and enhance the effectiveness of influencer campaigns.

Expansion to Emerging Platforms:

1. TikTok and Short-Form Video: The explosive growth of TikTok and the popularity of short-form video content will continue to reshape the influencer marketing landscape. Brands will increasingly leverage TikTok influencers to reach younger audiences and capitalize on the platform's creative and viral nature.

2. Live Streaming and Ephemeral Content: Live streaming platforms like Twitch, Instagram Live, and YouTube Live will become integral to influencer marketing campaigns. Brands will collaborate with influencers to host live events, product launches, and Q&A sessions, capitalizing on the real-time engagement and authenticity of live content.

Evolution of Measurement and Analytics:

1. Focus on ROI and Performance Metrics: Brands will demand more robust measurement and analytics capabilities to evaluate the effectiveness of influencer campaigns. The emphasis will shift from vanity metrics like reach and impressions to more meaningful metrics such as engagement, conversions, and return on investment (ROI).

2. Advanced Attribution Models: Improved attribution models and tracking technologies will enable brands to better attribute conversions and sales to influencer-driven touchpoints across the customer journey. This enhanced visibility into campaign performance will enable brands to optimize their influencer strategies and allocate resources more effectively.

Regulatory and Ethical Considerations:

1. Transparency and Disclosure: Regulatory scrutiny around influencer marketing will continue to increase, leading to stricter guidelines and requirements for transparency and disclosure. Influencers and brands will need to ensure compliance with regulations regarding sponsored content, endorsements, and disclosures to maintain trust and credibility with their audience.

2. Ethical Brand Partnerships: Consumers will expect influencers to be more discerning and selective about the brands they partner with, prioritizing ethical considerations

such as sustainability, diversity, and social responsibility. Influencers who align with brands that share their values and demonstrate genuine commitment to ethical practices will resonate more strongly with their audience.

In summary, the future of influencer marketing will be characterized by the rise of micro-influencers, emphasis on long-term relationships, integration of new technologies, expansion to emerging platforms, evolution of measurement and analytics, and increased focus on regulatory and ethical considerations. By staying abreast of these trends and developments, brands and influencers can adapt their strategies to thrive in an ever-changing digital landscape.

Emerging trends and technologies shaping the industry

Emerging trends and technologies are continuously reshaping the influencer marketing industry, providing new opportunities for brands and influencers to connect with audiences in innovative ways. From advancements in content creation to shifts in consumer behavior, these trends and technologies are influencing how influencer marketing campaigns are planned, executed, and measured. Here are some of the key emerging trends and technologies shaping the industry:

Short-Form Video Platforms:

1. TikTok: TikTok has quickly become one of the most popular platforms for short-form video content, particularly among Gen Z and younger millennial audiences. Brands are increasingly leveraging TikTok influencers to create engaging and viral content that resonates with these demographics.

2. Instagram Reels: Instagram's response to TikTok, Reels, is gaining traction as a platform for short-form video content. Influencers are using Reels to showcase their creativity, entertain their followers, and collaborate with brands on sponsored content.

Live Streaming and Ephemeral Content:

1. Live Streaming: Platforms like Twitch, YouTube Live, and Instagram Live are becoming increasingly popular for influencer-led live streaming events, Q&A sessions, and product launches. Live streaming allows influencers to engage with their audience in real-time and create authentic, unfiltered content.

2. Ephemeral Content: Platforms like Instagram Stories and Snapchat offer opportunities for influencers to share ephemeral content that disappears after 24 hours. Brands are collaborating with influencers on sponsored Stories to create authentic and engaging content that feels native to the platform.

Augmented Reality (AR) and Virtual Reality (VR):

1. AR Filters: Influencers are using AR filters on platforms like Instagram and Snapchat to create interactive and immersive content experiences. Brands can collaborate with influencers to develop custom AR filters that promote their products or enhance their brand messaging.

2. VR Experiences: VR technology is enabling influencers to create immersive storytelling experiences that transport audiences to new virtual worlds. While still in its early stages, VR holds promise for influencer marketing campaigns that seek to engage audiences in unique and memorable ways.

AI-Powered Content Creation:

1. Content Generation: AI-powered tools and platforms are making it easier for influencers to create high-quality content at scale. From automated video editing to AI-generated captions and thumbnails, these tools streamline the content creation process and enable influencers to focus on creativity and storytelling.

2. Audience Segmentation: AI algorithms are helping influencers better understand their audience demographics, interests, and behaviors. By leveraging AI-driven analytics, influencers can tailor their content to resonate more

effectively with their target audience and optimize their engagement and reach.

Influencer-Owned Products and Brands:

1. Product Lines: Influencers are increasingly launching their own product lines and brands, leveraging their personal brand and audience trust to drive sales. From beauty products to fashion lines, influencers are monetizing their influence by creating products that align with their niche and audience interests.

2. E-commerce Platforms: Influencers are partnering with e-commerce platforms to sell their own branded merchandise directly to their audience. By integrating e-commerce functionality into their social media channels, influencers can create seamless shopping experiences for their followers and monetize their influence more effectively.

Niche and Micro-Influencers:

1. Niche Audiences: Brands are increasingly targeting niche audiences and demographics by collaborating with influencers who have highly specialized interests or expertise. Niche influencers, also known as micro-influencers, often have smaller but highly engaged

followings within specific niches, making them valuable partners for brands seeking to reach targeted audiences.

2. Hyper-Local Influencers: Hyper-local influencers are gaining prominence as brands seek to connect with audiences at the community level. These influencers have a deep understanding of local culture, events, and trends, making them effective advocates for location-based marketing campaigns.

Data Privacy and Regulation:

1. Data Protection: With growing concerns about data privacy and security, influencers and brands are facing increased scrutiny around how they collect, use, and share personal data. Compliance with data protection regulations such as GDPR and CCPA is becoming essential for influencer marketing campaigns to maintain trust and transparency with audiences.

2. Regulatory Compliance: Influencers and brands are navigating a complex landscape of regulatory requirements related to sponsored content disclosures, endorsements, and transparency. As regulators crack down on deceptive marketing practices, influencers and brands must ensure compliance with guidelines from regulatory bodies such as the FTC and ASA.

Sustainability and Social Responsibility:

1. Ethical Brand Partnerships: Influencers are increasingly aligning with brands that demonstrate a commitment to sustainability, social responsibility, and ethical practices. Brands that prioritize environmental stewardship, diversity and inclusion, and social impact are resonating more strongly with audiences and influencers alike.

2. Purpose-Driven Campaigns: Purpose-driven marketing campaigns that support social causes and charitable initiatives are gaining traction in the influencer space. Influencers are using their platform to advocate for important social issues and drive positive change in their communities, aligning with brands that share their values and commitment to social impact.

In summary, the influencer marketing industry is evolving rapidly, driven by advancements in technology, changes in consumer behavior, and shifts in regulatory and ethical considerations. By staying informed about emerging trends and technologies, brands and influencers can adapt their strategies to engage audiences effectively, drive meaningful impact, and stay ahead of the curve in an ever-changing digital landscape.

Opportunities and challenges for influencers in the years ahead

As the influencer marketing landscape continues to evolve, influencers will encounter both opportunities and challenges that shape their careers and impact their success in the years ahead. By understanding these dynamics, influencers can capitalize on opportunities while navigating potential obstacles effectively. Here are some of the key opportunities and challenges for influencers in the years ahead:

Opportunities:

1. Diverse Revenue Streams: Influencers have the opportunity to diversify their revenue streams beyond brand sponsorships, including affiliate marketing, product sales, memberships, and digital products. By leveraging multiple income streams, influencers can create more stable and sustainable revenue sources.

2. Niche Specialization: Niche and micro-influencers have the opportunity to capitalize on their specialized expertise and interests to connect with highly engaged audiences. By focusing on specific niches and verticals, influencers can establish themselves as authoritative voices and attract loyal followers who share their interests.

3. Authentic Brand Partnerships: Influencers have the opportunity to collaborate with brands that align with their values and resonate with their audience. By prioritizing authenticity and relevance in brand partnerships, influencers can maintain trust and credibility with their

followers while creating meaningful content that drives results for brands.

4. Creative Freedom: Influencers have the freedom to express their creativity and individuality through their content, allowing them to connect with their audience in authentic and compelling ways. By embracing their unique voice, style, and personality, influencers can differentiate themselves and stand out in a crowded digital landscape.

5. Community Building: Influencers have the opportunity to foster a sense of community among their followers, creating a supportive and engaged audience that feels connected to their brand. By nurturing relationships with their audience and facilitating interactions and discussions, influencers can cultivate a loyal and dedicated fan base.

Challenges:

1. Saturation and Competition: The influencer landscape is becoming increasingly saturated, with more creators vying for attention and opportunities. As competition intensifies, influencers may struggle to stand out and differentiate themselves from the crowd, requiring them to find unique angles and niches to capture audience interest.

2. Algorithm Changes: Platforms frequently update their algorithms, impacting the visibility and reach of influencer

content. Influencers may face challenges in adapting to algorithm changes and maintaining consistent engagement and growth on social media platforms, requiring them to stay informed about platform updates and adjust their strategies accordingly.

3. Monetization Pressures: Influencers may face pressure to monetize their platform and generate income, leading to potential conflicts between commercial interests and authenticity. Balancing brand partnerships and sponsored content with maintaining audience trust and credibility can be challenging for influencers, requiring them to prioritize transparency and disclosure in their collaborations.

4. Regulatory Compliance: Influencers must navigate a complex landscape of regulatory requirements related to sponsored content disclosures, endorsements, and transparency. Compliance with regulations such as the FTC guidelines and local advertising standards is essential for influencers to maintain trust and transparency with their audience and avoid potential legal consequences.

5. Burnout and Mental Health: Influencers may experience burnout and mental health challenges due to the pressures of maintaining a consistent presence on social media, managing brand partnerships, and dealing with criticism and scrutiny from followers and peers. Taking steps to prioritize self-care, set boundaries, and seek support when needed is essential for influencers to sustain their well-being and longevity in the industry.

In summary, influencers face a range of opportunities and challenges in the years ahead as they navigate the evolving influencer marketing landscape. By leveraging their creativity, authenticity, and expertise, influencers can capitalize on opportunities to engage and connect with their audience while addressing challenges such as competition, algorithm changes, and regulatory compliance. By staying informed, adaptable, and resilient, influencers can navigate the complexities of the influencer industry and continue to thrive in the years ahead.

Epilogue: Your Journey to Influence

Reflecting on your progress and achievements

Reflecting on your progress and achievements as an influencer is an essential practice for personal and professional growth. It allows you to celebrate your successes, acknowledge your growth, and identify areas for improvement. By taking the time to reflect on your journey, you can gain valuable insights into your strengths, weaknesses, and goals, helping you to chart a course for future success. Here's why reflecting on your progress and achievements is important, along with some tips for how to do it effectively:

Importance of Reflection:

1. Celebrating Milestones: Reflecting on your progress gives you the opportunity to celebrate your achievements and milestones along the way. Whether it's reaching a certain follower milestone, securing a significant brand partnership, or launching a successful product line, taking the time to acknowledge your accomplishments boosts morale and motivation.

2. Learning from Experience: Reflection allows you to learn from your experiences, both successes and failures. By analyzing what worked well and what didn't, you can identify patterns, insights, and lessons that inform your future decisions and strategies.

3. Setting Goals: Reflecting on your progress helps you set realistic and meaningful goals for the future. By understanding where you stand currently and where you want to go, you can create a roadmap for achieving your aspirations and objectives as an influencer.

4. Maintaining Perspective: In the fast-paced world of influencer marketing, it's easy to get caught up in the day-to-day hustle and lose sight of the bigger picture. Reflection allows you to step back, gain perspective, and assess your journey from a broader standpoint, helping you stay grounded and focused on what truly matters to you.

Tips for Effective Reflection:

1. Set Aside Dedicated Time: Schedule regular periods for reflection in your routine, whether it's weekly, monthly, or quarterly. Find a quiet and comfortable space where you can relax, unwind, and engage in introspection without distractions.

2. Journaling: Keep a journal or digital notebook where you can jot down your thoughts, reflections, and insights. Write about your recent achievements, challenges you've overcome, lessons you've learned, and goals you want to pursue in the future.

3. Review Your Content: Take time to review your past content, including blog posts, videos, and social media posts. Analyze which pieces resonated most with your audience, what topics generated the most engagement, and how your style and approach have evolved over time.

4. Seek Feedback: Reach out to trusted friends, mentors, or fellow influencers for feedback on your progress and achievements. Their perspectives can offer valuable insights and provide a different lens through which to view your journey.

5. Practice Gratitude: Cultivate an attitude of gratitude by reflecting on the blessings, opportunities, and support you've received along the way. Expressing gratitude for your successes and the people who have helped you along your journey fosters positivity and resilience in the face of challenges.

6. Visualize Your Future: Take time to visualize your future aspirations and goals as an influencer. Imagine where you want to be in one year, five years, or ten years from now,

and reflect on the steps you need to take to turn your vision into reality.

Acknowledging Growth and Progress:

1. Celebrate Achievements: Take time to celebrate your achievements, no matter how big or small. Whether it's reaching a follower milestone, launching a new product, or receiving positive feedback from your audience, celebrate your successes and the hard work that went into achieving them.

2. Recognize Personal Growth: Reflect on how you've grown and evolved as an influencer since you first started your journey. Acknowledge the skills you've developed, the challenges you've overcome, and the lessons you've learned along the way.

3. Embrace Challenges: Instead of viewing challenges as setbacks, see them as opportunities for growth and learning. Reflect on how you've navigated past challenges and the resilience and perseverance you've demonstrated in the face of adversity.

4. Stay Flexible: Remain open to change and adaptation as you reflect on your progress and achievements. Recognize that your goals and priorities may evolve over time, and be

willing to adjust your strategies and plans accordingly to stay aligned with your values and aspirations.

In summary, reflecting on your progress and achievements as an influencer is a powerful practice for personal and professional growth. By celebrating your successes, learning from your experiences, and setting goals for the future, you can continue to evolve and thrive on your journey as an influencer.

Setting new goals and aspirations for the future

Setting new goals and aspirations for the future is essential for personal and professional growth as an influencer. By defining clear objectives and aspirations, you can create a roadmap for your journey, stay motivated, and continue evolving as a creator. Whether you're looking to expand your audience, launch new projects, or deepen your impact, setting goals helps you focus your efforts and channel your energy towards meaningful outcomes. Here's how to set new goals and aspirations for your future as an influencer:

Reflect on Your Journey:

1. Review Past Achievements: Reflect on your past successes and accomplishments as an influencer. Identify milestones you've reached, challenges you've overcome, and lessons you've learned along the way.

2. Assess Strengths and Weaknesses: Evaluate your strengths, weaknesses, and areas for improvement as an influencer. Consider your unique talents, skills, and attributes, as well as areas where you may need to develop or refine your abilities.

3. Consider Audience Feedback: Take into account feedback from your audience, peers, and collaborators. Reflect on what resonates most with your audience, what they value most about your content, and how you can continue to meet their needs and expectations.

Define Clear Objectives:

1. Set Specific Goals: Define clear, specific, and measurable goals for your future as an influencer. Whether it's reaching a certain follower milestone, launching a new product or service, or collaborating with a specific brand, articulate your objectives in concrete terms.

2. Prioritize Your Goals: Identify the most important goals and aspirations you want to focus on in the short term and long term. Prioritize your goals based on their significance, feasibility, and alignment with your values and vision as an influencer.

3. Break Down Goals into Actionable Steps: Break down larger goals into smaller, actionable steps that you can take to achieve them. Create a plan of action with specific tasks, deadlines, and milestones to keep you accountable and on track towards your objectives.

Expand Your Horizons:

1. Explore New Opportunities: Stay open to exploring new opportunities and avenues for growth as an influencer. Consider branching out into new content formats, platforms, or niches that align with your interests and expertise.

2. Collaborate with Others: Seek opportunities to collaborate with other creators, brands, and industry partners. Collaborative projects can help you reach new audiences, expand your network, and unlock new creative possibilities.

3. Attend Events and Conferences: Attend industry events, conferences, and workshops to stay informed about the latest trends, developments, and best practices in influencer marketing. Networking with other influencers and industry professionals can inspire new ideas and insights for your own journey.

Stay Flexible and Adapt:

1. Embrace Change: Recognize that your goals and aspirations may evolve over time, and be willing to adapt and adjust your plans accordingly. Stay flexible and open-minded as you navigate the dynamic landscape of influencer marketing.

2. Learn from Setbacks: View setbacks and challenges as opportunities for growth and learning. Instead of becoming discouraged by obstacles, reflect on what you can learn from them and how you can use them to become stronger and more resilient.

3. Celebrate Progress: Celebrate your progress and achievements along the way, no matter how small. Acknowledge the steps you've taken towards your goals and the effort you've invested in pursuing your aspirations as an influencer.

Stay Motivated and Inspired:

1. Find Inspiration: Surround yourself with sources of inspiration and motivation that fuel your creativity and passion as an influencer. Whether it's following other creators, consuming diverse content, or engaging with your audience, find what inspires you and drives you to excel.

2. Visualize Success: Visualize yourself achieving your goals and aspirations as an influencer. Imagine the impact you

want to have, the projects you want to create, and the legacy you want to leave behind. Use visualization techniques to stay focused and motivated on your journey.

3. Stay Consistent: Consistency is key to achieving your goals and aspirations as an influencer. Stay committed to your vision, and maintain a regular posting schedule, engagement with your audience, and progress towards your objectives over time.

By setting new goals and aspirations for your future as an influencer, you can create a clear direction for your journey, stay motivated, and continue growing and evolving as a creator. Whether you're looking to expand your audience, launch new projects, or deepen your impact, defining clear objectives helps you focus your efforts and channel your energy towards meaningful outcomes.

Encouragement and support for fellow influencers on their journey

Encouraging and supporting fellow influencers on their journey is not only a generous act but also a mutually beneficial one. In an industry often characterized by competition, fostering a spirit of camaraderie and collaboration can lead to stronger relationships, personal growth, and collective success. Here's why encouragement and support are essential for fellow influencers, along with some ways to offer encouragement and support to your peers:

Importance of Encouragement and Support:

1. Promotes a Positive Community: Encouraging and supporting fellow influencers helps foster a positive and supportive community within the industry. By lifting each other up and celebrating each other's successes, influencers contribute to a culture of mutual respect, camaraderie, and collaboration.

2. Provides Emotional Support: Influencer marketing can be challenging and demanding, with influencers facing pressure to maintain a consistent presence, engage their audience, and navigate the ups and downs of the industry. Offering encouragement and support provides emotional reassurance and solidarity to fellow influencers during difficult times.

3. Strengthens Professional Relationships: Building strong professional relationships with fellow influencers can lead to collaboration opportunities, networking connections, and mutual support in the industry. By nurturing relationships based on trust, respect, and encouragement, influencers can create a supportive network of peers who uplift and empower each other.

4. Fosters Personal Growth: Encouraging and supporting fellow influencers on their journey can also lead to personal growth and self-improvement. By sharing insights, experiences, and advice with each other, influencers can learn from each other's successes and challenges, gaining new perspectives and skills along the way.

Ways to Offer Encouragement and Support:

1. Celebrate Their Successes: Take the time to celebrate the successes and achievements of fellow influencers, whether it's reaching a follower milestone, securing a brand partnership, or launching a new project. Comment on their posts, send them a congratulatory message, or share their content with your audience to show your support.

2. Offer Words of Encouragement: Send words of encouragement and support to fellow influencers when they're facing challenges or setbacks. A simple message expressing empathy, encouragement, or solidarity can go a long way in lifting their spirits and motivating them to keep going.

3. Engage with Their Content: Show your support for fellow influencers by engaging with their content regularly. Like, comment, and share their posts, and tag them in relevant conversations and collaborations to help boost their visibility and reach.

4. Collaborate on Projects: Look for opportunities to collaborate with fellow influencers on projects, campaigns, or content collaborations. Collaborative projects not only strengthen professional relationships but also offer mutual support and exposure to each other's audiences.

5. Share Resources and Insights: Share helpful resources, tips, and insights with fellow influencers to support their growth and development. Whether it's recommending a helpful tool or sharing your own experiences and learnings, offering valuable advice can contribute to their success.

6. Provide Constructive Feedback: Offer constructive feedback and encouragement to fellow influencers on their content, branding, or strategy. Be supportive and constructive in your feedback, offering suggestions for improvement while highlighting their strengths and accomplishments.

Leading by Example:

1. Be Genuine and Authentic: Lead by example by being genuine, authentic, and supportive in your interactions with fellow influencers. Show sincerity and empathy in your words and actions, and strive to create a culture of kindness and encouragement within the industry.

2. Be Inclusive and Welcoming: Create an inclusive and welcoming environment for fellow influencers, regardless of their background, niche, or level of experience. Embrace diversity and celebrate the unique perspectives and talents that each influencer brings to the table.

3. Pay It Forward: Remember the support and encouragement you've received from others on your journey, and pay it forward by offering the same level of encouragement and support to fellow influencers. By lifting each other up, you contribute to a culture of generosity, collaboration, and success within the influencer community.

Encouraging and supporting fellow influencers on their journey is not only a generous act but also a mutually beneficial one. By fostering a spirit of camaraderie and collaboration, influencers can build stronger relationships, experience personal growth, and achieve collective success in the industry. Whether it's celebrating their successes, offering words of encouragement, or collaborating on projects, every act of support contributes to a positive and thriving community of influencers.

Conclusion

In conclusion, the journey to becoming an influencer is as diverse and dynamic as the individuals who embark upon it. Throughout this book, we've explored the multifaceted aspects of influencer marketing, from defining influence in the digital age to navigating the complexities of content creation, audience engagement, and brand partnerships.

Becoming an influencer is not just about amassing followers or securing brand deals; it's about authentically connecting with your audience, sharing your passions and expertise, and making a meaningful impact in the lives of others. It requires dedication, perseverance, and a willingness to embrace both the triumphs and challenges along the way.

As you embark on your own influencer journey, remember that there is no one-size-fits-all approach to success. Stay true to yourself, cultivate your unique voice and perspective, and never underestimate the power of authenticity in building genuine connections with your audience.

Embrace the opportunities for growth and learning, seek support and guidance from fellow influencers and mentors, and above all, never lose sight of your passion and purpose as you navigate the ever-changing landscape of influencer marketing.

Whether you're just starting out or looking to take your influencer career to new heights, remember that the most fulfilling journeys are often the ones that are fueled by passion, authenticity, and a genuine desire to make a difference in the world.

So go forth, dear reader, and embark on your influencer journey with confidence, courage, and conviction. The world is waiting to hear your story, and your unique voice has the power to inspire, educate, and uplift countless others in ways you may never imagine.

Here's to your success as an influencer, and to the countless lives you'll touch along the way.

www.ingramcontent.com/pod-product-compliance
Lightning Source LLC
Chambersburg PA
CBHW071211240526
45470CB00018B/1742